Kevin had a chop.

He got it from a shop.

He ran away to the top
of a hill with his chop.

He was hot.

He dropped his chop on an ant-hill.

Plop, plop, plop.

Look at the ants hop,
hop, hop.
They ran on Kevin.
"Stop, stop, stop."

Then Lotty went up to
the top of the hill with
a mop.

"Stop, you ants.
Stop, stop, stop.
Get off Kevin.
Mop, mop, mop."

So the ants put the
chop in the ant-hill.
Flop, flop, plop.

Kevin was sad.

He'd lost his chop.

The ants had got it with
the mop.